PIVOTAL
PERFORMANCE

7 Steps to Achieving Personal Excellence

DAVE FULLER · ALINA SHAKIROVA

tellwell

Tellwell Talent
www.tellwell.ca

ISBN
978-0-2288-7036-4 (Paperback)

Praise for
PIVOTAL PERFORMANCE:
7 STEPS TO ACHIEVING PERSONAL EXCELLENCE

You don't need to be a magician to reach Ideal Performance State – just read this book. It allows to create your own protocol and dramatically increase Performance in any field.

— Dr. Igor Zavialov, internationally recognized Health and Performance expert, Sports Medicine Physician, and Merited Coach of Russia

Congratulations on publishing this fantastic book. I like the practical exercises and your writing style. I will recommend it to others.

— Bernie Heine, President of Professional Business Coaches Inc, Business Coach and Sales Trainer, Massachusetts USA

Pivotal Performance is Very insightful, there is so much that can be used in sales and leaderships. This book presents some great opportunities for reflection.

— Chris Wall, Ford

TABLE OF CONTENTS

FORWARD

Walk into any car dealership, call center, gym or even a government office and you will find people who outperform their peers by 2 - 1 or higher in terms of results they achieve. As the owner of companies that have employed hundreds of people over the years, I (Dave) have always been fascinated by why some people work harder than others and why some people seem to achieve better results without seeming to work as hard. What motivates people to come to work, and keeps them working? I am particularly captivated when somebody seems thrilled to do a job I might find boring, tiresome or laborious.

I met Alina in the summer of 2020 when I was the assistant coach of the women's basketball team at the University of Northern British Columbia. I noticed Alina spent time before and after practice working on her skills; those workouts seemed to make a difference to her performance. One day Alina and I had a conversation regarding our common interest in this idea of personal performance, from which planted a seed from which this research and the resulting ebook was formed.

In our personal quests to better ourselves we all have examined our own personal performance, sometimes in appreciation, but other times with discouragement. We both know we could perform at a higher level in many of our personal activities, but like many of you, we have been challenged to figure out just how to take our performance to the next level.

In December and January of 2020-21 we conducted a small research study to learn about what personal performance means to people and the conditions that help people like you and I improve our outcomes. We wanted to provide valuable information to athletes and professionals in the workplace to help them achieve better results. We also believe this information would be of interest to company leaders who would like to understand what motivates top performers and how to create environments where people could excel in their roles at work or in the sporting arena.

We surveyed 125 professionals of different ages and from various backgrounds ranging from business owners and managers to athletes and sales professionals. Some of these people we sat with and asked in per- son, and many others answered online. From this research we obtained deeper insight regarding personal performance in the work setting. Moreover, some of our findings were consistent with psychology research conducted by large universities and published in journals. We hope you find the information in this book interesting and useful in your drive to perform at your highest level and help those around you achieve great things.

Dave Fuller   *Alina Shakirova*
Dave Fuller, MBA   Alina Shakirova

Chapter One

WHAT IS PERSONAL PERFORMANCE?

WHAT IS PERSONAL PERFORMANCE?

We all want to perform at our best. The fact that you are reading this right now suggests you have a level of interest in bettering your performance. But what exactly is personal performance?

Performance is defined as:

Consistent actions to fulfill your personal goals that are coherent with an organization's goals. Depending on the organization, performance may also include factors such as achieving targets, improving efficiency, reduction of costs, consistency of service, personal growth, and learning.

From this point of view, our performance is defined as achieving those goals we have set for ourselves. Outsiders, such as employers or coaches will be looking at our performance in light of how it aligns with the goals of the organization. A sports coach will be examining your individual level of results from the perspective of how it contributes to the team's goals. A sales manager might examine the performance of a sales professional from the point of view of how they are contributing to the sales of the company. However, just achieving results might not be the only factor that a coach, sales manager or leader considers when evaluating your performance.

When we surveyed people about what personal performance meant to them, the responses demonstrated that personal performance has different meanings to different people. These differences can account for the fact that respondents come from diverse backgrounds. However, despite these differences, there is still considerable overlap across responses. About 41% of respondents said personal performance meant achieving goals, accomplishing tasks, or getting things done. Yet nearly 20% of respondents mentioned "doing my best." Other common answers included efficiency and success at their jobs. Based on these responses, we see that for many people personal performance is about demonstrating results and being proactive.

Regardless of how people define personal performance, this concept is apparently an important part of their life. We found almost 60% of respondents think about their performance daily, while 25% of participants think about personal performance at least once a week. How often do you think about your performance?

HOW HAPPY ARE YOU WITH YOUR PERFORMANCE?

When I sat down with Peter to talk about how he felt he was doing in his job he told me he thought he was doing okay. When I asked him to explain more, he told me he really liked his job but felt he was struggling to get work done in a timely manner. He said he was worried about what his boss thought of his performance. If I had asked Peter how he would rank his performance on a level of 1-10, I am pretty sure he would have said about a 6.

How people evaluate a particular object might change depending on their mood, perceived pressures and what they are comparing it to. However, asking over a hundred people in a private setting about performance helped us see a general trend in how people evaluate themselves.

When asked how happy individuals are with their performance on a ten-point scale, most people (almost 90%) said they are pretty happy with their performance, evaluating it at 6 or above. The most common answers were 7 or 8, 30.9% and 28.5% of people, respectively.

While evaluating their performance at 7 or 8, people like you often commented that they are pretty satisfied with how they perform, but like Peter they felt there is still room for improvement. For some of you this comment might seem somewhat cliché, and make you wonder if there is any- one who is very happy with their performance. Indeed, 5% of people said they are very happy with their performance.

At this point you might also be curious how many people are unhappy about their performance. We found that about 11% rated their performance at 3/4/5. What we also found interesting is that people rarely say they are absolutely unhappy with how they perform.

Rate from 1-10 how happy you are with your performance? (where 1 is not happy at all and 10 is very happy)
123 responses

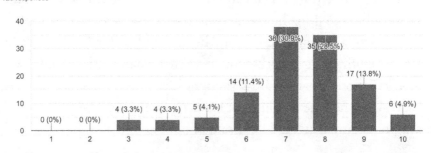

"The most splendid achievement of all is the constant striving to surpass yourself and to be worthy of your own approval."

– Denis Waitley

STEP 1: BE CLEAR ABOUT YOUR PURPOSE AND GOALS

It was a beautiful September evening when Mark Harasimiuk and I, along with three friends from Ireland, drove out into the woods to hike up to a remote forestry cabin for the weekend. Neither Mark nor I had been to the cabin at Raven Lake, but being in our 20's and eager to impress our Irish guests we were enthusiastic about our prospects of making the cabin before it got too dark. We found the start of the path as the sun was setting, but the 3 hours following were a comedy of errors, including losing the trail and realizing we didn't have the right equipment for a hike that was much more difficult than we first imagined. We discovered the cabin only by accident after we caught a reflection of the full moon off a woodshed's metal roof.

Unfortunately for most of us, we are travelling towards unknown destinations in our lives without a map. We might have an idea of where we want to end up, but usually we haven't planned properly and may only reach that destination with some luck. In many cases we don't even follow a path, we just head out to accomplish something and get lost on the way. It is difficult to perform at our best if we are disoriented, confused or simply lost. In order to perform optimally, it is proven we need to have clarity about where we are going and how we are going to get there.

Because you are trying to improve your own personal performance you might be interested in how others describe their best performance. **What do they feel like when they are at their peak? Under what conditions do people demonstrate their best performance?** If you are like us, you probably would like to know how to get in that zone to be the best you can be each and every time.

We discovered that the key to performing your best is having clarity about what you are trying to achieve. Whether completing a report, serving customers, or playing your best at a given sport, without clearly understanding your objective, it is difficult to perform at any level of satisfaction. The top performers in any arena have clarity about their goals; they know what they are trying to accomplish and why they are working so hard at it.

Unfortunately for most sales professionals, athletes, business owners, managers or employees, there is a tremendous lack of clarity about what we want to achieve either personally, athletically or professionally. Occasionally we might come across a person who has an understanding about what they want to achieve in a certain aspect of their life, however it is rare to find some- one who has done the work to define what they want to accomplish in all the necessary aspects.

While some people seem intrinsically motivated, there is a huge gap for many people around why they should attempt to perform at their best. As a result, most people are just mediocre in their performance of roles and tasks. This is generally due to the fact many people are not clear about their personal reasons for attempting to achieve outcomes.

THE FIRST STEP TO GOALS SETTING – DEFINING YOUR GOALS

At Pivotleader we work to establish clarity with all our clients early on in the relationship, in order to support them in achieving their dreams. To do this we ask them to write down and share their key goals with us. We are often amazed to hear that many of these successful people have never taken the time to write down what they want to be doing 1 year, 5 years or 15 years down the road.

Like most people these professionals and entrepreneurs are floating along in life hoping to get somewhere without realizing where that somewhere is. The amazing fact is that this goal setting or planning doesn't need to take a lot of time. It's been said that whether you take 3 days or 30 minutes to write down your goals, there will not be much significant difference. As we discussed earlier, while the time you spend writing down your goals might not matter, performance will improve as a result of that activity.

In order to achieve clarity of what you want to accomplish with your life, we encourage people to think about what they believe is their purpose. Why are you here? For some people this is a difficult exercise, while others can verbalize it clearly after a couple minutes. If you are able to define your purpose it is easier to relate why you are trying to achieve certain goals.

Someone like you might say they believe their purpose is to be a light for the people around them and in order to do that they want to be an Olympic athlete, or a weekend warrior. You might be able to justify their goals in a number of different ways, and each person will be different, however, they might say if they can be an example for others, they will have achieved their purpose.

A salesman might believe that his purpose in life is to be a great father or spouse, and his goal is to sell the most gadgets in his company so he has the money to fulfill that goal. Taking time to think through this can be challenging and you don't need to feel guilty that you are unsure of your purpose in life. The understanding of your purpose may change as you change. **However, we challenge you right now to write down a couple sentences or a few words about what your purpose in life is.**

My Purpose...

Once we have a purpose, and it need not be perfect, we are ready for the next step of setting goals. The goals don't always need to be attached to the purpose, but having the framework of understanding of your purpose in the back of your mind may change the way you look at goals. For example, if you feel your purpose is to make people happy, you might play sports or do a hobby to enable you to have a great outlook on life. If you are happy then others around you will likely have a great chance of being influenced by your happiness.

PURPOSE AND PROFESSIONALS – ESTABLISHING GOALS IN THE WORKPLACE:

In order to get better results for our teams, as coaches and managers we start by asking questions to understand clearly what is motivating our team members in order to help them to understand themselves and the reasons why they should work to perform at their highest levels.

One reason for mediocre performance is that as coaches and business leaders we don't provide clear objectives or goals for our team. We communicate in vague and uncertain ways about what we want our people to do. We might say we want to win, or make customers happy, or make a profit. What our players and employees need is clarity about what it means to win or succeed or profit. Does winning mean beating a few teams or taking home the championship? What does it mean to have a clean workspace, or happy customers? As you can see those are very hard to define, yet as individuals we set goals like that for ourselves. "To be the best I can be." "To do an awesome job." These are meaningless as they offer no tangible definition of success.

Our own experience with our teams and clients is that goal setting is key to optimal performance. We hypothesized early on that the use of goals would be instrumental in successful people achieving great results. As we can see from the survey, this idea that people are using goal set- ting as a method of improving their performance was substantiated. We asked the question, "Do you set goals?" An overwhelming majority of people, 87%, said yes, they are setting goals. 6% said sometimes Only 7% said no.

When we asked people about the kind of goals they set, we found people set various goals: long-term, short-term, specific, more general, work or life-related. One common trait of all these goals is that most of them are result-oriented. However, as research shows, it is highly beneficial to set process and learning-oriented goals along with the result-oriented goals. Additionally, it was interesting to see that 41% of people relate good performance to achieving goals, and some respondents suggested that setting goals helps them perform better.

The second problem affecting performance when it comes to goals is that we often fail to implement steps to ensure we achieve that goal. A quote we like states, "A goal without a plan is just a dream." Many people only achieve a small percentage of what they could truly accomplish because they believe that they know what they want and know how to get it. However, failing to follow certain steps to ensure their success often results in dreams that are never realized.

Do you set goals for yourself?

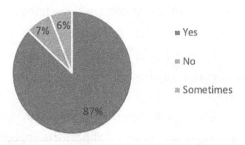

DOES GOAL SETTING REALLY WORK?

Scientific research shows that by writing down your goals your chance of success is increased significantly. In a revealing study by Dr Gail Mathews of Dominican University (Matthews, 2007), of over 260 Business owners and professionals in the US and worldwide, there was a significant difference in the success rate between people who just stated their goals and those who actually wrote their goals down and provided weekly updates to a friend.

This is how the study worked. Participants were broken down into five separate groups.

- Group #1 just thought of the business-related goals they hoped to accomplish over the period of the next month rated those goals in terms of difficulty, importance and the resources they had and needed to accomplish the goal.

- Group #2 did the same but wrote down their goals.

- Group #3 wrote down the goals and their actions steps towards the goals.

- Group #4 wrote down the goals their action steps and sent these commitments to a friend.

- Group #5 went further than any of the other groups and sent a weekly progress report to a friend.

So what happened next is what typically happens to business owners when they just think of goals but don't make concrete plans to follow through.

By the end of the four week study, only 43% of Group #1 had accomplished their goals or were halfway to completing them. Compare this to the business owners in Group #4 who wrote down their goals, made action steps and told a friend about them. This group accomplished or were more than halfway to completing 64% of their goals.

Finally, if we look at Group #5 who were sharing their goals and giving progress reports to be accountable, we see that a whopping 76% of goals were actually completed or half way there. This not only goes to show that writing down goals works but also that being accountable to those goals can make a significant difference in actual performance achievements.

A more recent 2019 study published in the Journal of Contemporary Education, by Michaela Shippers et al, found that university students who wrote down their life and school goals improved their performance by 22% over a similar cohort that had no goal setting exercise where goals were written, shared and visualized.

A SIMPLE EXERCISE TO SET GOALS AND ACHIEVE CLARITY

Goal setting seems simple in theory but in practice it is rarely done. Working with athletes and companies it is shocking to see how few actually set tangible goals that are written and referred to on a regular basis. Unfortunately, this is due to the fact that we often don't have a practical process for documenting our goals. The result is companies and individuals that are rudderless in their direction.

With organizations, setting direction and goals is usually accomplished with the implementation of 5-year strategic plans and the use of 90-day planning to back up those longer term goals. With individuals, there isn't the same required process from stakeholders to get results. This means that as individuals we are left to our own devices which for many people is nothing, unless of course we were brought up in a family that discussed such matters.

If you are serious about your performance you will want to set some long term and short-term goals. Long term goals might be 5, 10 or 15 years depending on your age. Short term goals will likely be 1 year and perhaps supported by a 90-day plan.

When writing down our goals it is important that we imagine ourselves in that future time. We want to start sentences with words such as "I am..." or "I have..."

For example: In 5 years I have $50,000 dollars in the bank. I have been recognized as the top athlete in my sport in this region. My team sees me as a great leader and often tells me I have made a difference in their lives. I have achieved the top seller of the year 3 years in a row. I have paid off my line of credit. I am going on regular weekly dates with my wife. I go to the gym 3 days a week.

SMART Goals

To get the best results, we want to make the goals SMART: Specific, Measurable, Achievable, Realistic and Timely. It's no use writing down frivolous goals we know are totally unrealistic However, unless we dream a little we will never have anything to set our sights on and achieve. It is amazing what can be accomplished by setting your mind to something that others might think is unachievable but you know in your heart that you are willing to put the time and energy into completing it!

DO IT NOW - 15 Minutes to Get Clarity on What You Want to Achieve

Grab a pen and three sheets of paper (or print out the Goal Exercise below). Using your phone, set a timer for 2 or 3 minutes. At the top of each page write 1 year, 5 years and 15 years and that future date.

Start your timer, and as you think about the time frame you are working on, imagine how old you are and start each sentence with the words, "I am" or "I have." Some people prefer to do point form, this works too, however it is best if you start each point with "I am" or "I have" to help your brain picture what you are trying to achieve.

This exercise should take 10-15 minutes tops!

Once you are finished with your 15-year plan, follow it up with a 5 year and then a 1-year plan. If you have a shorter time frame or think it might be too repetitive to do three worksheets, just do a 1-year plan. Set your timer and go again.

ULTIMATE GOALS EXERCISE

Today's date: Name:

My Physical/ Athletic/ Health Goals

My Spiritual, Emotional, Mental Health Goals

My Lifestyle Goals

My Financial Goals

Business, Sales and/or Workplace Goals

SO YOU HAVE SOMETHING ON PAPER

Congratulations! You have completed the first step in improving your personal performance. If you were to do nothing else, it is empirically proven that because you now have clarity on your ultimate goals there is a statistically significant chance that you will get better results in your performance than the person sitting next to you in your office, or the athlete standing beside you as you practice your chosen sport.

At this point you can do two things:

1. Either share your goals with someone you trust or

2. Fold. up your paper and put it away in a drawer somewhere so that you will stumble across it in a few months.

As the Matthews study showed, you are far more likely to have greater success if you are accountable! Share it!

CHAPTER TWO

THE CRITICAL ESSENTIALS – DEVELOPING A PLAN

STEP 2: THE CRITICAL ESSENTIALS – DEVELOPING A PLAN

In order to perform at our best, we each have personal factors that influence our performance. For example, on the basketball court, Alina might be focused on 3-5 critical essential factors that she believes ensures she plays at her best. For Alina these are:

1. Touching the ball each and every time she is on defence.

2. Following through on her shot.

3. Focusing on her footing as she is taking a shot.

4. Spending time before and after each practice working on her shot.

While other basketball players might have different critical essential factors that will make a difference in their performance, Alina knows when she is focused on these four things there is a greater chance she is going to have a great game. If she has a great game each and every time she is on the court she will have a much better chance of achieving her 1 year goal of being a scoring leader. She knows that if she is a scoring leader she will have a higher chance of achieving one of her ultimate goals of playing professionally.

Each of us has these critical essential factors that affect our performance. As a business coach and a consultant Dave has critical essentials he needs to focus on daily which he believes will help him achieve his ultimate goals of making a difference in the lives of leaders, their employees and their families for generations to come.

1. Listening closely to each and every client when they are in front of him.

2. Helping clients get clarity on what they need to do to overcome their biggest immediate challenges or take advantage of their opportunities.

3. Ensuring that the client receives significant value and can verbalize that value.

4. Blocking appropriate time each day for meditation, exercise and family.

When he was running his retail business, Dave's daily critical essentials were different than those of a business coach, they included:

1. Walking through the store and spending a few minutes with each manager and staff member every day.

2. Spending time each day working the floor for at least an hour to understand what customers were looking for and what the trends were.

3. Checking in on the business's 90-day plan to see how it was progressing.

4. A salesperson we know told us the three things that make the biggest difference for him:

5. Counting the number of No's he receives in a given day.

6. Talking to at least 25 customers a day by phone or in person.

7. Watching closely for signals in the conversation that the customer is ready to take the next step.

Unfortunately for most of us, we rarely take time to think about those tasks that are critically essential to our success. These processes that ensure the task gets accomplished with the desired outcome are critical to its success. Yet most of us never spend the time to analyze what those processes are. This analysis need not be laborious. You probably already know what con- tributes to your success.

When we asked survey respondents what factors contributed to their success, we received answers like "getting enough sleep," "making sure I am in the right mindset," "being focused," and "managing my time." However, these are vague and ineffective because for most of us we haven't thought through exactly what it is that makes the difference.

Yes, sleep and nutrition and attitude are foundational in success and we will need to be focused on those aspects of our life to ensure we can achieve our dream to be the best we can be. However, if we really want to be successful in our performance we need to take it a step further.

Each of us in our position has specific things we know lead to us performing at our best. One thing to note is that our idea of what is our best is going to be different from anyone else. We are all raised differently with different values, understandings and expectations. Some of this is cultural and some of this may be as a result of our experiences. This is why when it comes to the critical essentials that enable us to perform at our best, the essentials will differ.

WHAT ARE YOUR CRITICAL ESSENTIALS?

When you can understand the key factors that influence your success, you can focus on them daily to ensure that you hit your goals. It doesn't matter if you are a doctor, lawyer, man- ager, entrepreneur, athlete or student. There are several things that you know make a difference to your performance. If we were to ask surgeons what was critical to their successes in the operating room, one surgeon might say, "Feeling the presence of the knife in my fingers and standing squarely on the floor," where another surgeon in the same hospital might say, "Slowing down my breathing and having a feel for the energy of the patient, while relaxing and having some fun with the support staff."

Same operation, same hospital, different critical essentials that are important to being successful and getting a similar result.

YOUR TURN! WHAT ARE THE CRITICAL ESSENTIALS TO YOUR SUCCESS

Take a few minutes here to write down those factors that make the biggest difference to your success. Depending on your focus, you may need to write down your Critical Essentials for different aspects of your performance.

For example, Dave's critical essentials when he is selling or coaching are different from his critical essentials when he is focused on writing articles or those things that are essential when working with a company to create a strategic plan.

Alina's critical essentials will be different for her academic endeavors compared to her basket- ball endeavors.

In order to get your best results, break down some of the key areas of those activities where you want to improve your performance and find the critical essentials for each.

Activity #1

Critical Essentials	#1
	#2
	#3

Activity #2

Critical Essentials	#1
	#2
	#3

Activity #3

Critical Essentials	#1
	#2
	#3

CHAPTER THREE

FAKE IT TILL YOU MAKE IT!

YOUR SELF IMAGE AND ITS EFFECTS ON YOUR PERFORMANCE

"We play golf against par – something clear, a standard, to measure against. But we play life against ourselves. While striving for better, more, higher, or whatever adjective we use in our life's work – we are our harshest critic. It is true; we know our every fault, every failing, and every character shortcoming. We need not wear every flaw on our sleeve. We need to let our actions do our talking for us, let our internal compass guide our deeds, and not worry about what our critics have to say most importantly, that one internal critic who knows us the best."

— Mark Kolke

Believe it or not, your performance is limited.

However, that limitation to what you can do with your life, in your job or in your sport is primarily defined by you and your mind and not by outside factors.

Take for example Roger Bannister, who broke the record for the 4-minute mile in 1954, probably long before you were born. Roger had been told, as had all athletes for the decade before, that it was physically impossible, even dangerous, to run a mile or 1.6 KM in under 4 minutes. In fact, the record remained at 4.01 minutes for over 9 years, and gifted athletes and their coaches had taken the 4-minute mile as a challenge since 1886. So after almost 70 years of global effort to break the record, how did Roger Bannister break it and why is it now that even high school athletes, gifted ones of course, manage to break 4 minutes on a regular basis?

Roger Bannister was no doubt a gifted runner. He competed in the Olympics in 1952 and came 4th in the 1500m after which he decided he would put his mind towards breaking the 4-minute mile. He trained specifically to break the record and recruited others around him who also believed it could be done. On a cold windy day in 1954 Bannister did what many people thought would never be possible: he broke the 4-minute mile with a time of 3:59.4.

Once Bannister broke the record, the 4-minute mile no longer stood as a mental barrier for other runners. In fact just 46 days later an Australian runner John Landry broke Bannister's record with a time of 3:58 for the mile. Within a year numerous other runners had all broken what was perceived to be insurmountable.

So what does this have to do with your performance you might be asking yourself. **The truth of the matter is that our bodies will master what our brains believe is possible.** Most people never perform beyond the limits of the way we see ourselves and those limits are what we focus on each and every day. A great example of this is the case where George Danzig, a math student, showed up late for a high-level university Math exam. Three questions were written on the board. George completed the first two quite easily but the third one took more time and he finished it with just minutes to spare.

It turns out that the third question was the instructor's example of a math problem that "couldn't be solved" Einstein himself had been stumped on how to solve it. Because he had come in late, George Danzig wasn't told the question was "unsolvable", because he missed the introduction to the exam. In his mind he was supposed to find the answer and so he did.

We are consistently setting limits for ourselves and we don't even notice. How many times have you set a limit based on your age, your income, your family or culture of origin, your sex, some-one's commentary on you, or even a mark you got for some of your work in elementary school?

It is unfortunate that we let our minds get in the way of what we could possibly achieve. Yet it happens for each of us daily. If we want to live an extraordinary life, we need to start believing that we are extraordinary. We need to figure out a way to trick our brains into believing that we are great, that we can overcome obstacles and achieve our goals and dreams no matter how large they are.

In order to achieve greatness, we need to pretend that we are successful. Fake it until you Make It. Think back to your greatest accomplishments: my guess is if you are like anyone else, you probably started on the road to that accomplishment with nothing more than just an idea - a thought that perhaps one day something might change. You didn't understand the effort that would be involved, and the energy you would have to put into the tasks to ensure you would be successful. Yet you stuck with it, and the concept of what success looked like grew until one day you achieved something that was only a dream. Perhaps the results amazed yourself and those around you.

Now think about what you want to accomplish: you have dreams and goals for yourself writ- ten down, or at least clearly imagined. You know what is needed to achieve those goals. Why not start by seeing yourself as the person who can achieve that greatness?

Self Image Statements: Whether you want to be a superstar leader, salesperson, athlete, spouse, parent, engineer, or rocket scientist, the key to being successful is believing in yourself. A self image statement is one of the best ways to do this. By creating an image of what you want to become you are on the road to success.

Here are a couple examples of what a self image statement might look like:

"I have talent and drive and I am the best shooter on the team."

"My employees think I am the best boss they ever had because I care and spend time each day making sure they have the tools to do their job correctly."

"I am the top salesman in the company and my customers keep coming back to me because I give them special attention, they know I want them to get great results."

> **Your Turn! Write your own self-image statement as it pertains to your area of focus for performance.**

You may not be the best boss, best shooter, or top salesman now, yet this is exactly what we need to be telling ourselves if we are going to fake it until we make it. How we see ourselves is what we will become. If we continue to focus on our failures instead of what we want to become, our lives will never achieve the greatness that we are destined to accomplish. Having a positive self-image can be the difference between high performance and mediocre performance in all aspects of our life.

Author Robert White, a famous crime fiction writer, suggested to his readers:

"My invitation to you is to begin living every moment as though you are miraculous and deserve to live an extraordinary life. Fake it if you must and keep faking it until it's real to you. The gift you will be giving yourself is a lifelong journey of discovery, one that is infinite and infinitely rewarding. Begin the journey. Today. This moment. Now."

CHAPTER FOUR

REWARDING YOURSELF

WHY REWARDS ARE SO IMPORTANT TO YOUR PERFORMANCE

How often do you celebrate your successes? When was the last time you took the time to reflect on an achievement or treated yourself because you accomplished something that didn't seem possible for you before?

If you are like most people, you are so caught up in the daily routine that you probably don't stop and celebrate. We work hard to accomplish our goals but as quickly as we achieve the target we set for ourselves we move on and set another and another. As a result, oftentimes, we get little satisfaction from our accomplishments and in the end ask ourselves, what was it all for?

You have undoubtedly heard of Pavlov's dogs, who would start to salivate when they thought of the food they were going to eat. Our brains too have a way of getting excited if we think we are going to be rewarded. Yet we are talking about more than the constant stimulus we get from our cell phones or gaming apps. We are talking about the need to train our brain to get excited at the thought of getting a reward for improving our performance. When our actions or behaviour are rewarded by a pleasant outcome, we are more likely to try to repeat that action. Rewarding ourselves for positive results has been proven to work for both athletes and professionals alike.

A study much more recent than Pavlov's 1880 science experiments was done by Cornell researchers Woolley and Fishbach and published in the Journal of Personality and Social Psychology in 2018. These researchers found that when people were rewarded for achieving benchmarks in their work, performance improved, engagement improved and people were happier to try to achieve positive outcomes long after the rewards were gone.

Unfortunately, organizations regularly set goals for their employees and rarely celebrate when they achieve those goals. Whether we are hitting sales targets, or financial profitability targets or customer satisfaction scores, many leaders forget that we are intrinsically motivated to dwell in our success and that our teams get frustrated when we constantly demand more but give lip service to the efforts they have contributed to realize these goals.

Sports teams by their nature are more apt to celebrate successes even with small rewards such as high fives, cheering, celebration parties, trophies and awards. This provides incentives for team members to drive themselves to be the best they can. The culture of celebration is fantastic for those who are able to push themselves to be good enough to win. However, rarely do teams placing fourth in contests celebrate their successes. Instead they tend to dwell on their failures.

We know that the brain wants to give us more of what we focus on, so if we are focused on our failures, our debts, and our misery, our brain will find ways to give us more of that. When we are focused on our successes, our wins, and celebrations, our brains work hard to produce more of those endorphin rushes.

But what if we are not on a team that celebrates success? What if our goal is just making the team, getting through a project, putting a certain amount of money in the bank, or achieving success in our personal field? The good news is that there are still ways we can take advantage of the research that shows that rewards work to improve performance. As individuals we need to consider how we are going to reward ourselves for jobs done well, targets hit, or performances beyond our expectations.

Consider now what you would reward yourself with if you were to hit one of your larger goals? What would you like to give yourself as a prize? Would it be a trip, a day off, or dinner with friends? The bigger the achievement the bigger the reward! But that is totally up to you. The key here is that rewarding yourself will set the stage for the next goal.

You may have some intermediate targets on the road to your ultimate goals. How would you like to reward yourself for these? How about rewarding yourself for a great practice or a good month, or even for every sale along the way? These could be as small as giving yourself a walk around the block, a special drink or snack, or a meditation break.

In order to perform at our best, we need to give ourselves valid reasons to succeed. Rewarding ourselves upon completion of our tasks with something that we will enjoy helps us to concentrate on the tasks necessary for our success. It is one more way of helping us at our best each and every day of our lives.

Your Turn! How do you want to reward yourself for your achievements? Make a note of some small and large rewards that you would really enjoy. Tie these rewards to specific goals you have set for yourself previously.

CHAPTER FIVE

WHAT YOU ARE WILLING TO SACRIFICE?

STEP 5: CONSIDER WHAT YOU ARE WILLING TO SACRIFICE TO ACHIEVE YOUR GOALS

One of my biggest regrets is that I didn't stop home for a quick visit more often when my kids were young and my wife was stuck at home minding them. Because I was so tied up in managing and growing my business, I missed family meals, vacations and days off. If you are a leader serious about your organization, or an athlete serious about your sport, you have probably made this sacrifice too, as has your family.

There is a price to pay for every action we take. Your desire to perform at your highest level means you are going to have to sacrifice something in order to achieve your dreams. Most of us go through life without considering the cost of our drive to accomplish our goals. However, every time we choose to put effort into something, that energy cannot be put into something else.

For example, consider a leader who spends those extra hours before and after work to achieve the success they desire for their organization. Those extra hours at work are hours that they are not spending with their family or their friends. Those hours are time that is never going to be spent on leisure, travel, hobbies or exercise. Time spent in pursuit of a goal has a cost not only for the leader but it is also a sacrifice for their friends and family who are supporting them.

The athletes who are spending time at the gym perfecting their sports are missing out on time with their friends at the restaurant or park. They have chosen to spend time working out. As a result, they are sacrificing their time that might be spent studying, or travelling, to get closer to their dream fitness or skill level. Their family might have sacrificed thousands of dollars for them to achieve their performance goals.

A sales professional who is travelling to hit targets for the company that provides the family with extra money to live their dream lifestyle, is missing out on birthday parties, and leisure time which is being spent in an automobile or airport lounge. Yet the sacrifice is not only theirs but also anyone who has put in time, energy or effort to get them to this stage in life, including the customers who are meeting with them.

When we have clarity about what we want and what we believe we are called to do, we also need to be clear about what we need to sacrifice to achieve the plan we have laid out. We must recognize that when we are spending time living our dream and working to achieve our goals, no matter what they are, there is a cost. We need to understand what sacrifices are involved and who is making the sacrifice.

This also brings us to the point that if there is a cost to what we are doing, are we justified in using that time and energy for improving our performance?

Consider the fact that the time we spend watching the latest series on television is time we will not have to pursue our passions and achieve our goals, to make the world a better place through our work or actions. We have a choice on how we spend our time and our energy and the question always remains: "Did we spend it in the best possible way?"

Think about the time you spend as an athlete in the gym, the leader in the office, in a relationship, or perhaps as a salesman on the road. Are you really expending the necessary effort to achieve your goals? Remember, this is what you have been striving for. Are you focused or are you just wasting time? Are you honestly giving this task the required energy and focus? Are you attentive and present in your work?

I encourage you to consider what sacrifices are being made--by you and others--for your success. Is the sacrifice worth all that effort?

> **Take the time right now to write down what you are willing to sacrifice and give up in order to achieve your goals. Be specific in naming what you are going to miss out on.**

CHAPTER SIX

UNDERSTANDING YOUR IDEAL PERFORMANCE STATE

STEP 6: UNDERSTANDING YOUR IDEAL PERFORMANCE STATE

We know that if you have played any sports in your life, there has been a time when you felt like you were "in the zone" and executed precisely how you were taught. Wouldn't it be nice to be able to be so focused each and every day?

When I (Dave) was 18 years old, I hitchhiked 450 miles to play water polo in a tournament for a team that was short a player. En route, I had to spend a night sleeping on the floor at a home in a village in northern British Columbia courtesy of some people who were nice enough to offer me hospitality. When I got to the tournament, I was exhausted. Yet once the games started I was re-energized and wanted to impress my new teammates. I knew that I hadn't put all the effort into coming to this tournament just to sit on the sidelines. I wanted to impress. I was focused and knew my purpose was to help my team win, I had to score. I had the tournament of my life. Over the course of four games I scored 23 goals, putting me in the top 2 players of the tournament. I received an offer to play for a university as a result.

While I never took the offer to play water polo at a higher level, I felt this tournament was the peak of my water polo performance. I was on my game and felt like I couldn't miss the net when I took a shot. You know how that feels!

Consider right now a time when you felt like you were on top of your game, whether it be at work or in your sporting endeavors.

Being a perfectionist (Alina, definitely not Dave), I used to set very high (possibly even unrealistic) expectations for my performance and focused mostly on the desired outcomes: winning a game, scoring 25 points and achieving my set goals. I also thought that the best strategy to achieve those expectations was to become very pumped before the game, which did not work very well and as a result I was often disappointed. Why?

First, I had very high goals, but I was missing a critical component. I had no clarity about what exactly I needed to do to achieve those goals, the critical essentials. And as was discussed earlier, it is important to know what actions you need to take during your performance that will help you achieve the results you want.

Second, from an early age I learned that many great basketball players try to hype themselves up before the game to feel more excited and ready to go. For a long time I was convinced I had to do the same to play well, so I tried many different approaches to hype myself up before the game. However, I failed to notice that this approach did not work for me. I found it made me jittery, causing me to rush through my motions and make bad decisions, which negatively affected my self-confidence and, as a result, my overall performance.

Trying to hype myself up before the game resulted in me becoming tense emotionally and physically. I would feel like I was not allowed to have fun if I wanted to achieve my goals, which I realized now is the wrong way to think. In order to perform at our best we need to have fun and enjoy what you are doing. In fact research shows that when we are having fun we are more likely to have better results.

In the last few years, as I have focused on becoming a better athlete, I learned about the ideal performance state which is the body and mind balance at which people perform their best. That state is different for every individual.

Jason Selk, in his book "10 Minute Toughness," suggests that in order to achieve great results we need to consider our all time best performances and remember how aroused (physically and mentally) we were at those moments. Reflecting on my best performances helped me to realize that I played best when I was mentally in a relaxed, slightly uplifted mood, and not worried about expectations. Physically I had to be charged, but not tense. Therefore, I was able to see that previous approaches I used in pregame preparation moved me further away from my ideal performance state and limited my ability to achieve my ultimate goals.

Understanding how I feel in my ideal performance state has definitely helped me to perform better, and minimized some unnecessary stressors. I believe this approach will help you perform at higher levels as well.

SO WHAT EXACTLY IS THE IDEAL PERFORMANCE STATE AND HOW CAN YOU ACHIEVE THIS STATE EACH AND EVERY DAY?

The ideal performance state (IPS) is an optimum body and mind state that facilitates one's peak performance. More specifically, it refers to how physically energized and emotionally excited an individual is at a particular moment. The level of arousal can be depicted as a continuum, from being half asleep to being in a panic mode. The optimum level depends on each individual per- son and the task they are performing.

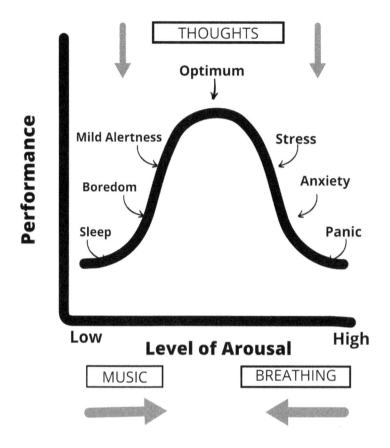

Knowing the benefits of understanding your personal IPS inspired us to include relevant questions in our survey. We asked people about situations in which they tend to perform better, and their preferred level of arousal.

About one-fifth of participants said they perform better when they are physically rested and in a good mental state (being focused and having positive attitudes). Once again, people mentioned that having clarity about tasks and goals, being prepared, and minimizing distractions greatly benefits their performance. For some people, being challenged also promoted better results. However, many people said stress and pressure should be of a moderate or low level in order for them to perform at their best levels.

We asked people to rate on a scale of 1 to 10 (where 1 is half asleep and 10 is running 100 miles an hour) how "hyped up" they were when they performed their best. Here are the results:

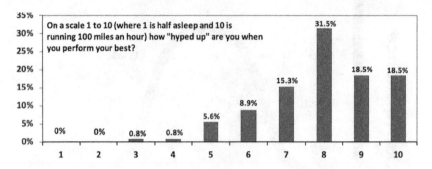

As you can see, everyone has their own ideal performance level. Just as Alina realized that being calmer helped her get better results, a significant proportion of respondents (over 40%) felt that they needed to be energized in the 9 or 10 range to get their best results. Unfortunately the research we did wasn't able to go deeper and compare the answers of high performers against their peers to determine if there are optimal levels of performance states. However we can leave that research for someone else!

Your Turn: Think about yourself, how hyped up are you when you perform your best? The following questions might help you to understand your ideal performance state:

1. How much pressure is enough and how much is too much?

2. How do I feel mentally and physically when I am at my peak?

3. How jittery or calm do I need to be to get my best results?

On a scale of 1 to 10 (where 1 is half asleep and 10 is running around 100 miles an hour), how "hyped up" are you when you perform your best?

Your Answer:

Describe in words your Ideal Performance State:

CONSISTENCY - TRUST - PERFORMANCE

Every organization and team has one, the star performer who consistently delivers results day after day, week after week, month after month and year after year. Occasionally this person will have a bad game or bad month, but they know how to get back on track and deliver again. Contrast this to the performance of most of us which is often mediocre and inconsistent. We have a good month followed by a bad month and then a mediocre performance.

While most professionals aspire to demonstrate their peak performance, not everyone worries about doing so consistently. However, we all want to be seen as trustworthy and accountable employees, managers, or athletes. It will give us a chance to be chosen to make the final shot or close a big sales deal. The more accountable and trustworthy we are in the eyes of our bosses, customers, and coaches, the more opportunities we receive. Each opportunity we get is another chance to achieve our goals.

Consistently putting in effort, focusing on your critical essentials and delivering the expected results will enable you to perform consistently at your best. This consistency will bring you closer to your end goals. Inconsistency of results, while it may be the start to a promising career in our chosen field, can be frustrating for us, our teammates and our leaders. When this inconsistency happens, your boss or coach will know that you are capable of doing well, but they will not be fully confident to trust you. On the other hand, if your boss and coach know that you consistently put in the effort and hard work, and get consistent results, trust will grow and the opportunities you have to perform will grow as well.

CONSISTENCY – *THE QUALITY OF ALWAYS BEHAVING OR PERFORMING SIMILARLY, OR OF ALWAYS HAPPENING IN A SIMILAR WAY*

ACCOUNTABILITY – *BEING RESPONSIBLE FOR WHAT YOU DO AND ABLE TO GIVE A SATISFACTORY REASON FOR IT, OR THE DEGREE TO WHICH THIS HAPPENS*

Not only do we have to build trust in others, we need to have trust in ourselves. I was working with a business owner recently who was afraid her business was going to fail. She had built up a successful business over the past 20 or so years and the recent economic challenges had left her feeling hopeless that the business could recover. She told me she felt she couldn't trust her decisions or her customers wouldn't come back. I could commiserate: in the year 2000, our two-year-old second business was in trouble, I had lost 272,000 dollars in the first year and 70,000 dollars in the second. I had lost confidence in my decision-making and that I was in the right place as leader of the company.

In hindsight, that struggle was exactly what I needed. The losses, the challenges, the pain, sorrow and difficulties, while hard to accept at the time, enabled me to learn the skills I would need for future endeavors. I was forced to trust my team, which grew with me and supported our customers and each other when I didn't have the energy or focus. I grew in my relationships with my family because I had to trust them with my weaknesses and I learned that they would be with me during my darkest hours. I trusted my partners and while their trust might have been shaken they learned to trust that I would see things through. While it was extremely difficult, I was forced to believe there was a bigger picture, a purpose that was beyond my control.

Research shows that trust builds better performance. In her study, Ana Costa (2003) found that trust is an important condition for perceived work performance, commitment to the organization and overall team functioning. In other words, trust is highly associated with better performance in individuals and teams. Trust between you and your manager often reduces the need for micromanaging, which according to our survey is one of the factors that negatively impacts performance (being mentioned by almost 12% of respondents).

Imagine what your life would be like if you were more consistent in your results? What is it that you need to do to achieve results more consistently? The trust resulting from this consistency is one part of a circle affecting performance, including consistency, accountability, trustworthiness and performance enhancement.

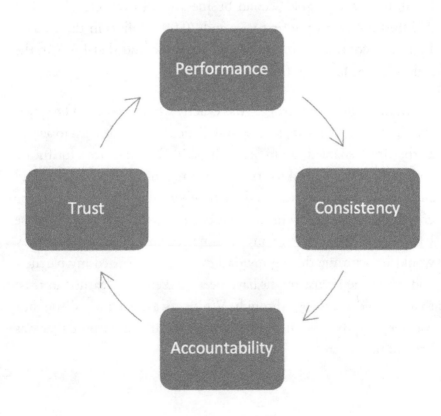

DO YOU HAVE INCONSISTENT PERFORMANCE?

Sherry sells cars, she is clear that the reason she sells is because she wants to support her son and have money for opportunities to spend time together. She has an idea of what she believes are her critical essentials and she tries to focus on these daily.

Unfortunately, Sherry's results are inconsistent. One month she might sell 10 cars, the next 6 and then the third month she might sell 12 vehicles. Her best month ever was 18 cars. This is challenging for her managers because they believe that Sherry has the potential to be a top seller, however they cannot trust that she will deliver day after day and month after month. This is limiting her access to the best leads and she is missing out on some opportunities that top sales professionals in her company might have.

The great news is that even inconsistent results give us an understanding of our potential. We might have a great day, super game or fantastic month, but when we learn to repeat those results time and time again, we get closer to fulfilling our ultimate goals.

We are all human beings, and our lives are not perfect. In whatever we do, it is very rare for our performance to follow a completely straight line. More often, it looks more like an intermittent line; some people describe it as stairs. It is normal to experience fluctuations in our performance over time; we are not robots. However, there are two important caveats about these fluctuations. It is all right if:

1) In the overall picture, you keep moving towards your goals; and

2) These fluctuations are not frequent and dramatic.

In other words, we want to avoid showing outstanding performance and then dropping to poor performance. Naturally we might have some off days, but by focusing on our critical essentials and having clarity of our goals and how we are going to reach them we will reduce these huge fluctuations in performance.

Additionally, we want to consistently improve our performance while minimizing the frequency of our bad performance. Thus, to achieve your goals in the most efficient way, to build trust in yourself and those around you, ideally you want your performance to follow the line depicted on the graph marked by a star and avoid the one marked with lightning.

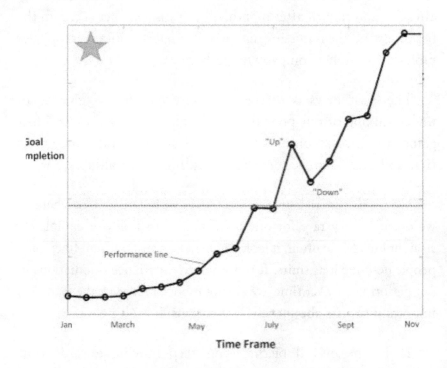

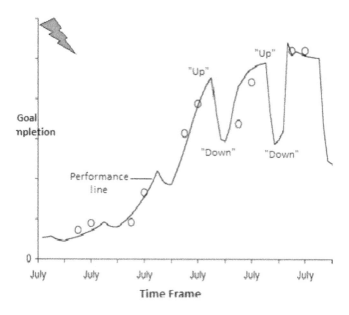

WHAT STANDS IN YOUR WAY TO CONSISTENTLY PERFORM AT YOUR BEST? STRESS, MINDSET AND PERFORMANCE!

In our curiosity to discover why some people are consistently excellent while others are consistently inconsistent we asked, "What stands on your way to consistently perform at your best?" The most common barriers to consistency, mentioned by 47% of respondents, are uncontrollable external factors, such as irrelevant/unnecessary questions and tasks, angry customers, overall distractions and no clarity.

Your thoughts affect your consistency!

Another significant factor, mentioned by 31% of respondents, is a negative mental state, particular anxiety, excessive worries, low motivation, and negative emotions. Other factors mentioned are low energy/physical tiredness (14%), very high volume of demands (13%) and poor time-management (13%).

We discussed earlier the need to have control over your thoughts. While it is difficult to do, high performers work daily to ensure they are on the right track. Understanding your ideal performance state and being able to put yourself in that state each time you are required to perform will help you achieve more consistent results.

Managing our stress can be difficult. In today's fast-paced world stress is a common part of our lives. What we find stressful is defined by our subjective interpretation of the situation (Lazarus, 1984). What might be stressful for you might not be the least bit stressful for another teammate or the person sitting next to you at work. Yet stress affects us all.

Do you remember a time in your life when you initially thought you would not be able to over- come a particularly difficult situation? We have all been there. Did you feel threatened and stressed at the time? If you are like most of us looking back in a rear-view mirror, once you achieved your goal, you realized it was not as big of a problem as you initially thought? You might even wonder why you worried at all.

I (Alina) remember such a situation. One season my team had to face a team ranked #1 in the conference (#3 in the country) in doubleheader games over the weekend. We lost the first game by an embarrassing 40 points but won the second one by 3. That season, this team ranked #1 had only one loss in their records, and it was from a small university in Northern Canada.

So what was the difference between these two games? The main difference was in our mind- set and how we approached these two games. Before the first game, we often heard we have no chance, and our goal was "not to lose by much." Ironically, that is exactly what happened in the first game. After the game, we had a team meeting and through that discussion we realized even though we played a great team, there was nothing incredible to be scared of. We had nothing to lose.

The next day, the first thing our coach told us during our morning pregame practice was, "Today, we want to give them a fight; we want to do our best and try to win the game." Going into the game with the belief that we want to do all we can and show our character enabled us to play much better. We played with great passion and executed our game plan, leading to a surprise win.

CONTROLLING STRESS AND USING IT TO ENHANCE PERFORMANCE

An interesting understanding of stress is that much of the time, people feel stressed when their self-image or performance is threatened. In our survey, most people (68%) admitted they experience stress related to their performance. This stress can be triggered by external factors (such as our bosses, clients, or colleagues) or internal factors (unrealistic self-expectations or negative self-image).

In our survey, 59% of individuals suggested their stress comes mostly from their thoughts and expectations. External factors were mentioned by 26% of people. Meanwhile, 15% believed the stress they experience comes from both external and internal factors.

How our beliefs and appraisal interact with our performance:

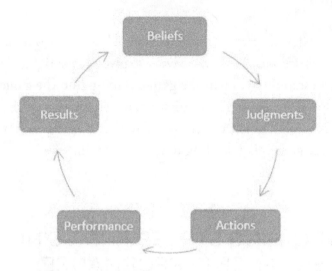

Did you know, according to research, Lazarus (1984), most of the time, your internal perception of a situation is what determines whether you will feel stressed or not. Our survey results support this stress model, as the majority of those who feel stressed about their performance admit it comes from their internal thoughts. Moreover, perceiving an event/problem as a threat activates the "fight or flight" response in your body (due to stress hormones release), which causes anxiety and tension.

Therefore, one way to reduce stress is to look at problems as a challenge rather than a threat. In this way you can stay calm, think straight and find the best possible solution to a positive out- come. Using this mindset will give you more confidence in your abilities to overcome these complicated demands, affecting your actions and performance.

CHAPTER SEVEN

TRACKING SUCCESS FOR BETTER OUTCOMES

STEP 7: TRACKING SUCCESS FOR BETTER OUTCOMES

By focusing on what is going right and not what is going wrong enables us to think differently and as a result have a different outcome. But how can we do that? Unfortunately, most organizations, teams and individuals rarely put thought or effort into daily accountability or regular journaling of success. It is true that in sports and sales we track our results, but rarely do we try to figure out the essential factors that make a difference to those results. In other words, we might track our sales, but we don't look closely at what contributed to that success. An athlete might track time or results but doesn't closely consider the efforts, energy, nutritional or mental preparation that made the difference.

The two regular actions you can do to affect your success are a daily success log and a weekly accountability check.

Daily success log. At the end of each workday or after a practice/game, take 3-5 minutes to think about (or even write down) three things you did well and three things at which you did not succeed much. Doing so will help you understand whether you executed what you initially planned, what you need to work on tomorrow and why you should feel good about yourself (because you found 3 things you did well!).

Weekly accountability check. At the end of every week, take some time to reflect on:

1. What is the best thing you enjoyed about your work this week?

2. What were the results of your activities this week?

3. In what ways did you move towards achieving your goals this week?

4. What did you learn last week?

5. What are you working on next week?

6. What are you looking forward to next week?

The best way to do your accountability check is to find a partner who you trust and might be on a similar path and work together keeping each other accountable.

WRAPPING IT UP: SIMPLE STEPS YOU CAN FOLLOW TO IMPROVE YOUR PERSONAL PERFORMANCE

As you probably recognize by now, excellence in performance involves much more than just achieving goals. Excellence in performance requires that we stay focused, committed, and confident in our approach. We need to recognize that we are faced with daily distractions and stressors that can affect our optimal performance. Of course, your personal performance also depends on factors, such as your preparedness, physical health, work environment, and clarity of the goals. It will also be dependent on good coaching of the basic skills you need in your sport or profession. This book therefore is a shorter version of a multifaceted approach to improving your performance.

The first step is to create clarity, which can be done by setting goals. Like any other activity, setting goals can be effective or ineffective. We gave you a goal-setting exercise that is constructed in a way that enables you not only to realize what you genuinely want to achieve but also how to do so. You gain clarity of what you need to do to become who you want to be. Take 10-15 minutes of your time to write down goals that will set you up for success. Make sure those goals are SMART.

The next step is to start acting like the professional you want to come. We talked about faking it until you make it. Internally we need to believe we are the person who can achieve those goals. The self-image you create will define how you go about your daily activities and challenges. In addition, remember how you should feel mentally and physically as you think about getting into your Ideal Performance State each and every time you go to perform your designated activity.

Every effort has a cost, and in order for you to perform at your best you need to make choices regarding your sacrifices. We also believe your brain needs to know that it is going to be rewarded for those sacrifices if you achieve your goals. What are those rewards?

Finally, most of the goals you set are long-term goals, and you need to realize that achievement of those goals doesn't happen overnight. They may take a long time and there are going to be considerable distractions along the way. Our consistent movement towards our dreams will continue to take us along the path to success. To avoid falling prey to inconsistency and procrastination, you can do three things.

First, review your goals every day in the morning and choose 2-3 critical essentials you want to focus on that day.

Second, at the end of each workday, consider having a success log that will help you to track your daily progress.

Finally, do not forget about your weekly accountability check. It will be more beneficial if you find an accountability partner to do your weekly check and enable you to see your progress through another set of eyes.

To make it easier for you, we summarized all these steps in our Personal Performance worksheet, which you can find at the end of this e-book.

Optimizing our personal performance can be a long and laborious process, but the fruits of our efforts are usually significant. We are sure you know of people who you consider to be successful and stand out from their peers. Their stellar performance might seem to come easy, however behind every overnight success are years of sacrifice by those stars and the people who have supported them. As you rise to stardom in your career and optimize your performance to enable you to achieve your dreams for your future we hope that this booklet energizes and reinforces your knowledge and gives you the fortitude to stick with those dreams despite the challenges you will face.

PivotLeader Personal Performance Worksheet

- Ultimate Goals:
- Annual Goal:
- Critical Essentials: What 3-5 things do you need to focus on daily to achieve your annual goals?
- My Self Image Statement:
- My Rewards:
- My Required Sacrifices:
- Ideal Performance State:
- Days I filled out my Daily Success Log:
- Did I fill out my weekly accountability check in?

Goals Worksheet

Today's date: Name:

Ultimate Goals
(5 Year Goal)

Annual Goals

Critical Essentials

What you need to focus on to achieve your annual goals

My Self-Image Statement

My Reward(s)   **Required Sacrifices:**

My Ideal Performance State today (1-10):

Days I Filled My Daily Success Log (circle):

☐ Mon ☐ Tue ☐ Wed ☐ Thur ☐ Fri ☐ Sat ☐ Sun

Did I Complete My Weekly Accountability Form?

Yes ☐   No ☐

CHAPTER EIGHT

PERFORMANCE IN A SLUMP? 5 THINGS YOU CAN DO TO REVIVE YOURSELF

PERFORMANCE IN A SLUMP? 5 THINGS YOU CAN DO TO REVIVE YOURSELF

I (Dave) bumped into Julie's father at the grocery store and inquired about how his daughter was doing in the business she owned, he told me that she was going through a rough patch. I made a mental note to call her and a few weeks later got Julie on the phone. The first thing I noticed was Julie's voice, the excitement was gone and her energy seemed depleted. She told me about everything that was going wrong, including dropping sales and a lack of customers. Julie told me that over the past few months she had felt defeated. She said that she felt like she was losing but didn't know why. Julie was in a slump!

Having worked with leaders and top performers in business and sport, it's apparent that each of us has times in our careers when we get into a slump. There are many reasons for slumps including emotional, physical, phycological, spiritual or economic factors. Slumps happen when we feel that we can't make shots, sales, or lead our teams effectively. As a manager or coach, it can be frustrating when we see one of our team get into a slump, but we recognize that people can't be at the top of their game all the time. Individually, we have all been through a general dry spell in our performance.

Here are 5 things you can do if you are in a slump!

1. **Mini Reset:** Often when we are in a slump it's because we have lost focus of our purpose. We have forgotten the love we have for what we do. As a result, we let external factors dictate how we feel or think. We end up putting too much

energy into worrying about factors that are beyond our control. In Julie's case she was more focused on customers that had left for economic reasons than focusing on the prospects that were walking right by her establishment each and every day. Sometimes a mini reset where we take the time to contemplate the reason why we are doing our job is all we need. A mini reset can enable us to regain our focus and purpose in order to meet our obligations whether they be payroll, lease payments, or our commitments to family or our team. Often a mini reset can be all the difference we need to get back on our game.

2. **Focus on 3 Essentials:** Leaders and Athletes in a slump can take for granted the focus and hard work it took us to achieve our high level of performance. Over time, we often become sloppy and let bad habits get in the way of our desired outcomes. When this happens, we need to get back to the critical essential factors of our success. What are the two or three things we need to do on a regular basis that drove our success in the first place? In Julie's case, her success built on the effort she had put into attracting new customers. She had previously spent time training her team to listen closely to customers, and she was creative in creating an experience for people walking into her business. As we discussed this, she realized that she had been putting less effort into these factors than she had in the past.

A basketball player I was working with recently who felt she was in a slump focused on her follow through, her footwork work, and put the time into practicing her shot. Reflecting on your previous success and the factors that have enabled you to get to where you are now can often inspire you to get back to the basics and on track.

3. **Be Honest and ask for help!** It's amazing that when we show our weakness as leaders, our teams will rally around and support us. Recently I had a family illness where I needed time off. When I expressed the fact that I couldn't do everything that was expected of me, friends, family and staff rallied to do what they could to help out. Admitting that you are in a slump and need some help will probably inspire your team to rally to your aid. Moreover, when you verbalize the challenges, you will often be surprised to hear that those around you already have recognized that you are at a low point and want to help.

4. **Consider a Sabbatical:** In 1994 I told my partner that I was taking a break from our business and booked 6 months off to travel the world. I came back refreshed and revitalized and as a result the business grew astronomically upon my return.

   Sabbaticals are a great way to overcome major slumps in your career. In 1998 Michael Jordan took a 18 month sabbatical from his basketball career. He came back to add a string of championships and records in the years that followed. Typically, a sabbatical is an extended leave from your job or business to refresh and revitalize. Most sabbaticals range from 6 months to one year and traditionally in some professions like academia are granted every 7 years. Unfortunately, in leadership we believe that we are expected to work throughout our career without any extended break. This lack of breaks often leads to professional burnout. If you are in a slump, consider this option seriously!

5. **Trust Yourself – Be Patient:** Your first professional slump can be confusing, however once you have gone through a dry spell, you will recognize that slumps are a natural part of life. It's impossible to perform at high levels continuously.

As professionals we need to be gentle on ourselves when we struggle. We also need to be patient. Often when we try to force our return to high levels, we become frustrated at our lack of results. This doesn't mean we should give up, instead we often have to go through the motions and trust that we have what it takes to return to our levels of success. The trust and patience we place will be rewarded in time if we give time a chance.

If you are in a slump, we feel for you. Having experienced a number of slumps at a personal and professional level, we know from experience that you will get through the experience and be better off for it. Slumps are one more bump in the school of hard knocks, learning how to get through them will make you a better leader and a better person.

Need Additional Help or Support?

Optimizing performance within an organization can be a challenge when team members are checked out or not contributing at their highest level. Unfortunately, there are limited resources for coaches or leaders to rely on that enable them to take performance to another level.

If you are frustrated by a lack of results, discouraged because of a dysfunctional team or tired of unmotivated team members, we encourage you to reach out to us to find out more about the training and support we offer to enable you to be the hero you are and lead your teams to achieving goals beyond their wildest dreams.

You can find more regarding our course information on our website www.pivotleader.com or by emailing alina@pivotleader.com. You can download PDF worksheets at pivotleader.com/worksheets

REFERENCE LIST

Accountability. Cambridge Dictionary. (2021). https://dictionary.cambridge.org/dictionary/english/accountability

Costa, A.C. (2003). *Work team trust and effectiveness.* Personnel Review, 605-622.

Consistency. Cambridge Dictionary. (2021). https://dictionary.cambridge.org/dictionary/english/consistency

Lazarus, R. S., & Folkman, S. (1984). Stress, Appraisal, and Coping. *New York: Springer.*

Matthews, D. G. (2007). The impact of commitment, accountability, and written goals on achievements. 87 Convention of the Western Psychological Association. Vancouver, B.C.

Performance. Cambridge Dictionary. (2021). https://dictionary.cambridge.org/dictionary/english/performance

Selk, J. (2009). 10-Minute Toughness: The Mental-training Program for Winning Before the Game Begins. *McGraw-Hill.*

Shippers, M. (n.d.). *We had a problem.* ERIM. Retrieved from https://www.erim.eur.nl/erasmus-centre-for-study-and-career-success/about-goal-setting/problem-results/

Woolley, K., & Fishbach, A. (2018). *It's about time: Earlier rewards increase intrinsic motivation.* Journal of Personality and Social Psychology, 877–890.

CPSIA information can be obtained
at www.ICGtesting.com
Printed in the USA
LVHW082054160922
728568LV00002B/383